MARTINA McBRIDE
WAKING UP LAUGHING

Alfred Publishing Co., Inc.
16320 Roscoe Blvd., Suite 100
P.O. Box 10003
Van Nuys, CA 91410-0003
alfred.com

ISBN-10: 0-7390-4905-4
ISBN-13: 978-0-7390-4905-1

CONTENTS

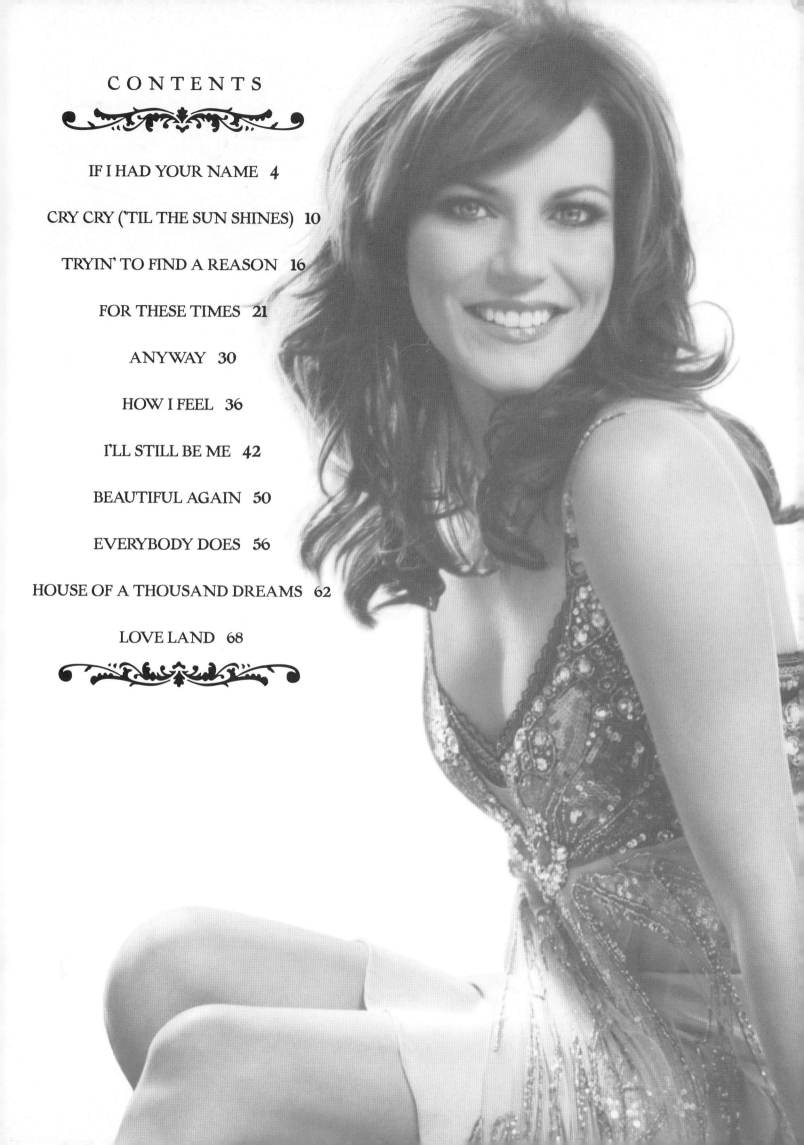

IF I HAD YOUR NAME

Words and Music by
HILLARY LINDSEY, STEVE McEWAN
and GORDON SAMPSON

If I Had Your Name - 6 - 1
28402

8

now.___

(Inst. solo ad lib....

CRY CRY

('Til the Sun Shines)

Words and Music by
MARV GREEN, CHRIS LINDSEY,
HILLARY LINDSEY and AIMEE MAYO

Moderately ♩ = 116

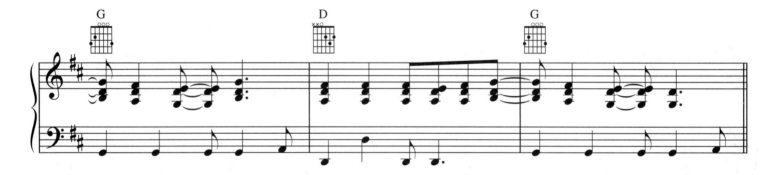

Verse:

1. I know a girl,___ she was a wait - ress.___
2. I know a man___ who tried to ease___ his mind,

right, ba - by._____
(Inst. solo ad lib....

...end solo)

14

TRYIN' TO FIND A REASON

Words and Music by
TOMMY LEE JAMES and JEREMY STOVER

Verse 1:

1. No love can sur-vive for long like this, when you're

stand-in' on a bridge that's al-ways burn - ing.

May-be it's just time to walk a-way, if you're

18

Is - n't this___ just point - less___ an - - y - way,   if you're
may - be that___ says all___ there___ is___ to say,   if you're

Chorus:

try'n' to find___ a rea - son to stay?___   It's hard to ad - mit it,   what
try'n' to find___ a rea - son to stay.___

we know in - side.___   We've tried ev - 'ry - thing,___   ev - 'ry -

To Coda

thing but good - bye.___   Say good - bye,___

20

FOR THESE TIMES

Words and Music by
LESLIE SATCHER

1. In these

Verse 1:

times in which we live,___ where the worst of what___ we live___ is

laid out for all the world___ on the front page,___ and the

Verses 2 & 3:

Verse 3:
For these times in which we live,
Seems like the only answer is
Givin' up on findin' one at all.
And we hide behind unsure,
Pull the blinds and lock the doors,
And hang a pleasant picture on the wall.
Blessed is the believer
Who knows love is our redeemer
And the only breath of life
For these times in which we live.
(To Bridge:)

ANYWAY

Words and Music by
MARTINA McBRIDE, BRAD WARREN
and BRETT WARREN

34

HOW I FEEL

Words and Music by
MARTINA McBRIDE, BRAD WARREN,
BRETT WARREN, CHRIS LINDSEY
and AIMEE MAYO

Moderately slow (♩ = 104)

I'LL STILL BE ME

Words and Music by
TAMMY HYLER and RACHEL THIBODEAU

Slowly, with feeling (♩ = 66)
Verse 1:

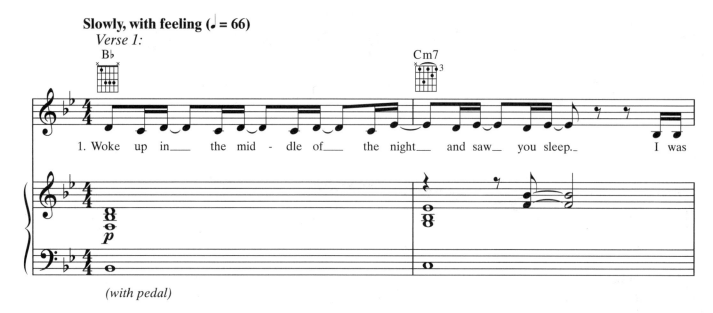

1. Woke up in__ the mid-dle of__ the night__ and saw__ you sleep.__ I was

(with pedal)

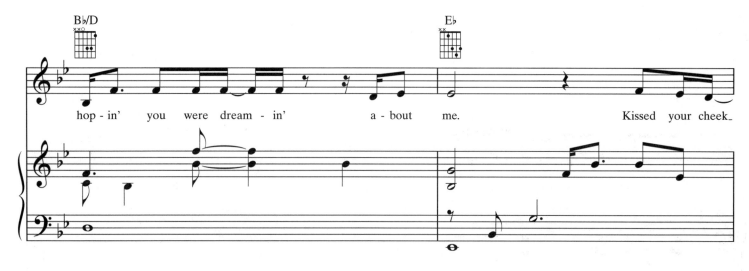

hop-in' you were dream-in' a-bout me. Kissed your cheek__

__ and said,__ "I love__ you," you reached for me__ and then__ you mum-bled, "I

I'll Still Be Me - 8 - 1
28402

Chorus 1:

Verse 2:

I'll Still Be Me - 8 - 6
28402

same girl that you've known___ for cen - tu - ries.

I'll still___ be___ me.___

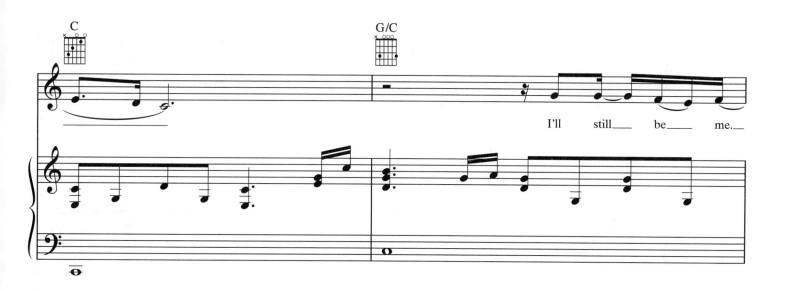

I'll still___ be___ me.___

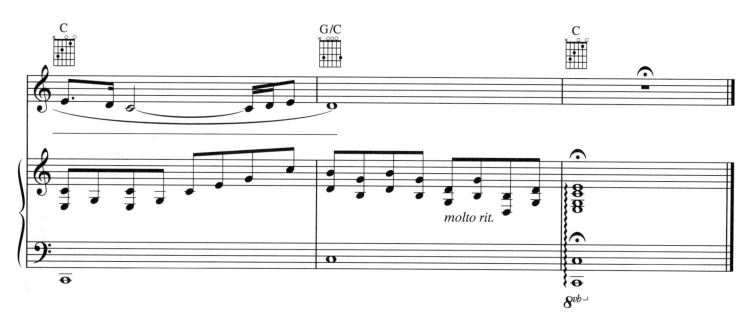

molto rit.

BEAUTIFUL AGAIN

Words and Music by
MARTINA McBRIDE, BRAD WARREN,
BRETT WARREN and NICK TREVISICK

52

3. Her boy-friend said I'm

Verse 3:

way too young to get mar-ried. But she made up her mind that some-how

she was gon-na find a way to keep that ba-by she car-ried. And he just walked_

Chorus:

a-way.

But when_ it rains,___

the past___ gets washed___ a - way,___ and___ then___ she smiles___ 'cause she___

___ knows in___ the end___ the world gets beau - ti - ful,___

beau - ti - ful___ a - gain,___ yeah.___

Interlude:

And when she 's ly - ing

Bridge:

Chorus:

EVERYBODY DOES

Gtr. tuned down 1/2 step:
⑥ = E♭   ③ = G♭
⑤ = A♭   ② = B♭
④ = D♭   ① = E♭

Words and Music by
DAN DEMAY, MIKE MOBLEY
and RACHEL PROCTOR

Verse:

1. This ain't the first___ time you've fall - en in love___ with your heart___ wide o - pen.___
2. How man - y times___ had you said, "He's the one,"___ and found out___ that he was-n't?

Feel - ing just___ like a fool,___ know - ing that you're the on-
Al - ways think - ing it's gon - na hurt for - ev - er, but then one___

* Cue notes apply to 2nd Verse.

Everybody Does - 6 - 1
28402

60

Everybody Does - 6 - 5
28402

HOUSE OF A THOUSAND DREAMS

Words and Music by
BILLY MONTANA, JENAI
and ILYA TASHINSKI

64

* Harmony vocal last time only.

House of a Thousand Dreams - 6 - 3
28402

LOVE LAND

Words and Music by
TOM DOUGLAS and RACHEL THIBODEAU

Love Land - 5 - 1
28402

Verse 3:

Verse 2:
Seemed like a lifetime driving from
Vegas to Oklahoma.
If you're allowed a number of mistakes in life,
Maybe I've filled my quota.
They called it a reception, saying we did the right thing.
And they smiled their broken smiles,
Said, "Who needs to walk down the aisle?"
And I showed off my wedding ring.
And we walked hand in hand to
Love Land.
Oh, how I love this man,
Love Land.